The Pocket Book of
HAPPINESS

The Pocket Book of
HAPPINESS
The bliss of being alive

ARCTURUS

With special thanks to Anne Moreland

ARCTURUS

This edition published in 2018 by Arcturus Publishing Limited
26/27 Bickels Yard, 151–153 Bermondsey Street,
London SE1 3HA

ISBN: 978-1-78950-094-3
AD006960UK

Printed in China

Introduction

Since ancient times, religious thinkers, philosophers, writers, and artists have reflected on how to achieve the balanced state of happiness and contentment that we all, as human beings, seek to attain. In this little book, we look at some of the ways they have suggested, adding the thoughts of many unknown individuals who have nonetheless contributed to our store of knowledge on this essential subject. Some of this advice is serious, some light-hearted; some profound, some funny. Together, the gems of wisdom you will find in these pages make up a guide to that most contradictory and elusive of human goals: happiness.

When we approve of ourselves, rather than always seeking approval from others, we find happiness.

When one door closes, another opens.

The path to happiness is paved with dreams, but don't forget to admire the beauty of the landscape as you travel.

Make your own happiness; it's up to you.

Don't spend your life looking back; remember the good times, but look forward to new ones.

If you make someone else happy, you make yourself happy.

Carpe diem –
seize the day.

Everyone has a different idea of happiness. Follow your own path, not someone else's.

We often make ourselves unhappy by wanting contradictory things in life.

Joy and sorrow come hand in hand.

Don't feel guilty if the things that are supposed to make you happy fail to do so.

Having achieved a special goal in life can make you happy, but there may also be a feeling of anti-climax – before you begin to aim for a new one.

You can't expect to be happy all the time. Human beings are not made that way.

A good, long soak in a hot bath will wash your cares away.

Make happiness your goal, and do whatever it takes to achieve it.

Don't try to define what happiness is; instead, think about what makes you unhappy, and try to change it.

Contentment is a pearl of great price, and whoever procures it at the expense of ten thousand desires makes a wise and a happy purchase. *John Balguy*

The sweetest moments are the shortest.

Slow down and enjoy life.
Otherwise you may forget
where you're going, and why.

**The smallest things in life bring happiness
– watch a flower grow, or a bird fly by.**

Happiness is contagious.

A person who is contented with what he has done will never become famous for what he will do.

Happiness has magical properties. It leads to long life, health, and resilience.

Contentment is natural wealth, luxury is artificial poverty. *Socrates*

Watching a bee take nectar from a flower you've grown is a happy sight to see.

Joy is a flower that blooms when you do.

Good humour is one of the best articles of dress one can wear in society. *William Thackeray*

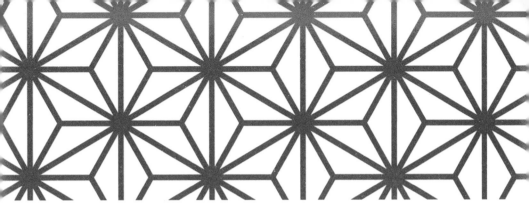

Contentment is being satisfied with things as they are, not as you would like them to be.

Feel, show, and express your happiness, so that others can share it, too.

Happiness is a natural outcome of being able to be oneself.

There is a connection between being grateful and being happy. But who knows which one leads to the other?

Happiness is a full belly.

Activities that involve us in the natural world – whether feeding the birds, stroking the cat, or going for a country walk – help us to feel happier.

Happiness is a decision, involving choice, action, and faith.

Don't envy other people's happiness – what makes them happy might not have the same effect on you.

Whenever you feel creative, playful, or silly, you are close to being happy.

Happiness is a state of mind that is open, friendly, and positive.

The original meaning of the word 'happiness' is 'good fortune,' or 'luck'.

Do not spoil what you have by desiring what you have not; remember that what you now have was once among the things you only hoped for. *Epicurus*

If you approach work with passion and energy, it will help you to be happy.

Happiness is an adventure. Set out on it.

There are many roads to pleasure, but only one true path to happiness.

Content makes poor men rich; discontentment makes rich men poor. *Benjamin Franklin*

Happiness is curling up with a good book beside a crackling fire on a cold winter's night.

Be content with your lot; one cannot be first in everything.
Aesop

Since we cannot always get what we like, let us like what we can get.

Some see darkness, misery, and despair in a rainy day: others, a sacred blessing from the heavens, refreshing us and giving life to all plants and creatures on this earth.

Happiness can see you. Can you see it?

Happy the man, and happy he alone, he who can call today his own; he who, secure within, can say, tomorrow do thy worst, for I have lived today. ***John Dryden***

To be happy in life, it helps if you don't think too much.

Happiness can make an ordinary sight beautiful.

The key to happiness is patience.

Happiness is not the fulfillment of what you want, but the realization of how much you already have.

A rich man is one who has no need of wealth.

Be yourself, with all your faults and strengths.

Don't let little things get you down. Keep a sense of perspective.

You will only fail if you stop trying.

It is important to feel valued. Stay close to those who value you, and distance yourself from those who do not.

In the war against fear, joy is the best weapon.

There are short cuts to happiness, and dancing is one of them. *Vicki Baum*

Conquer your fears by facing them. If you retreat, they will loom larger in your life.

You are a force of nature to be reckoned with.

If at first you don't succeed, you are just like everyone else. It's called learning.

Everyone deserves to be happy. It is within your power to become so.

Friendship is a cornerstone of happiness.

You can dance anywhere, if only in your heart.

Be careful what you wish for.

Trust yourself. Then you will know how to live.

Forgive your enemies – it will really annoy them!

Energy spent worrying is mostly wasted energy.

In the hustle and bustle of life, find a quiet place ... inside your mind.

Become absorbed in your activities, so that you are at one with what you are doing.

Don't wake up at night and worry. Wait until morning, when you'll find the problem has gotten smaller!

Solitude can be a friend and guide, leading you to happiness.

Learn to spend time with yourself.

Bringing love, luck, and happiness into your life takes hard work. It doesn't happen by itself.

Kindness costs nothing, and can bring so much happiness.

Never impose on others what you would not choose for yourself. *Confucius*

A walk, run, or any kind of exercise in the fresh air will help to brighten your day.

Dance first. Think later. It's the natural order.

Samuel Beckett

Cut down on multi-tasking. It tires the mind, and achieves little of value.

Give someone a 'gratitude gift'. Write down all the reasons you are grateful to them, and tell them.

Make a list of things that make you happy. You'll find there are more of them than you imagined…

Can you draw how it feels to be happy?

Take time to sit down and listen to a piece of music without doing anything else.

Anyone who says sunshine brings happiness has never danced in the rain.

The world is but a canvas to the imagination.

Henry David Thoreau

The art of happiness is like any other – the more you practise it, the better you get at it.

Happy people don't have the best of everything; they make the best of everything.

Happy are the painters, for they shall not be lonely. Light and colour, peace and hope, shall keep them to the end of the day.

Winston Churchill

Creativity is within everyone's reach – no exceptions. And to be creative, even in a small way, can bring great happiness.

Capture your daydreams. Keep them safely, and think of them often.

Criticism always cuts deep into our hearts. Praise often makes no impression at all. Learn to listen to the praise, as well as the blame.

Build a happiness habit. List five things per day that have made you happy.

Try to notice when you're happy.

If you respect yourself, you will not be so upset when others show disrespect for you.

When you feel overwhelmed by life's challenges, look back at the past and remember difficult times you've survived.

March on. Do not tarry. To go forward is to move toward perfection. March on, and fear not the thorns, or the sharp stones on life's path. *Khalil Gibran*

A kind heart and an open mind are the best travelling companions.

Feed your soul – meditate, walk by the sea, listen to music, visit art galleries and historic buildings. If you do, you'll feel more balanced.

Try to see the best in people.

The front left side of the brain is the part that registers happiness, wellbeing, and contentment. Make sure to exercise it!

Filter out your toxic language. Don't run yourself down, even to be funny. When you talk in negatives, you build a negative mindset.

Work connects us to others, building a happier world for everyone.

To find out what one is fitted to do, and to secure an opportunity to do it, is the key to happiness. *John Dewey*

Speak less, listen more.

Human beings are hard-wired for love and compassion.

Ask yourself, what are you grateful for? You'll find many answers.

Five keys to happier living: giving; relating; appreciating; accepting; questing.

Show affection, say thank you, and express what you value in friends, family, and workmates.

We cannot do great things on this earth – only small things with great love.
Mother Teresa

Fear closes down our minds and our hearts.

Constant criticism is highly destructive in relationships. For every negative comment, find five positive ones to add.

All growth depends upon activity. There is no development physically or intellectually without effort, and effort means work. *Calvin Coolidge*

Be present in all you do.

We are most true to ourselves when we're about nine or ten. So revisit that time in your life by taking up the hobbies that you enjoyed as a child.

Identify your strengths and weaknesses as a person. Then work on the strengths!

Action is the highest perfection and drawing forth of the utmost power, vigour, and activity of man's nature.
Bishop Robert South

Build some variation into your life. Take a different route to work, try food from a different culture, or visit a museum or gallery you've never been to before.

The only exercise some people get is jumping to conclusions, running down their friends, side-stepping responsibility, and pushing their luck …

Go confidently in your dreams. Live the life you have imagined. *Henry David Thoreau*

Our genetic make-up is thought to influence about fifty per cent of the variation in our personal happiness. The rest is up to us!

Giving money away makes people feel happier than spending it on themselves.

Reach out to help a friend in need – you can help them to see light at the end of the tunnel.

The journey is the reward.

Compassion is at the heart of happiness.

Make time to bring a friend flowers or a plant; to bake them a cake; or to send them an amusing link, or funny photo.

If you're feeling sad, don't pretend to be happy. Be yourself, and the mood will pass.

Well begun is half done. *Aristotle*

Set goals, big or small. Write them down. Be specific, rather than general.

The journey of a thousand miles starts with a single step. *Chinese proverb*

Don't expect to be a perfect person – acknowledge your mistakes, and move on.

You've got to find what you love and that is as true for work as it is for lovers … If you haven't found it yet, keep looking and don't settle. As with all matters of the heart, you'll know when you've found it. *Steve Jobs*

Celebrate success; take time to enjoy it, and thank those who helped you get there.

To everything there is a season, and a time to every purpose under heaven. *Ecclesiastes*

Ten minutes of meditation per day can help us be happier, more optimistic, and more spiritually aware.

At the heart of a happy relationship is good communication.

Challenge all thoughts that begin, 'What if …?'

Recognize your needs and the needs of others – that way you won't become tangled up in misunderstandings.

Beware of 'black and white thinking'. Ask yourself what is the worst that could happen, what is the best, and what is the most likely.

Giving support and receiving it from others helps us to be happy.

Think about how and when you experience feelings of happiness in your life. It's different for everyone.

Success has many fathers, while failure is an orphan.

Be genuinely pleased for others when things go well for them. It's not as hard as you think.

The only place success comes before work is in the dictionary.
Vince Lombardi

Be open to opportunity.

There is no happiness without struggle.

Never ignore your dreams for the future – they will help to guide you on your way.

When things go wrong, don't always blame yourself.

Don't pressure yourself to be happy. Instead, create a positive mindset: be open, appreciate, curious, and kind.

Let go of rigid expectations and expand awareness of natural beauty and human kindness.

All things are difficult before they are easy.

Thomas Fuller

Don't ask 'Why'? Instead, ask 'Why not'?

When we are young, we think we know everything. In old age, we find out we know nothing.

If one man kills a hundred men, and another masters himself, the second is the greater warrior.
Buddha

Kindness to others boosts happiness. It increases life satisfaction, provides a sense of meaning, and takes our minds off our own troubles.

A single moment of happiness can rub out hours of misery.

Turn the rocks in your path into stepping stones to help you along your way.

When you wake up in the morning, pause for a moment to honour the gift of another day.

The journey is the destination.

A cynic is a man who knows the price of everything and the **value of nothing.** *Oscar Wilde*

As you travel, don't forget to stop sometimes and admire the view.

The optimist turns problems into opportunities. The pessimist does the reverse.

Try to be polite in all situations, however annoying you find people – you will feel better for it.

Giving to others can be a simple kind word, or gesture.

Travel in your mind, as well as your body.

Your best may not be enough, but if you give of it, you will have no regrets.

Practise random acts of kindness.

Fear less, hope more
Whine less, breathe more
Talk less, say more
Hate less, love more
And all good things
are yours. *Swedish proverb*

If you never travel, you may be hiding from the adventure of the open road; if you make the open road your home, you may be hiding from the commitment of domestic life.

Treat each person you meet with respect – appearances may be deceptive.

Do not meet anger with anger. Count to ten, and ask yourself, why is this person so angry? If you pay attention, you may find out.

Respect is a form of love.

Don't let life pass you by. Live in the present, savouring each moment.

Acknowledge that you are special – there's no one quite like you.

Life is short, so don't waste a second of it!

Happiness is the greatest gift a person can have or bestow.

A sorrow shared is a sorrow halved.

To dwell on unhappiness is a waste of time. And wasting time is wasting life.

Live as if today might be your last.

When someone dies, at the exact same moment, a new person comes into the world. Thus the eternal cycle of life continues.

Do not base your happiness on material wealth. It can disappear all too quickly.

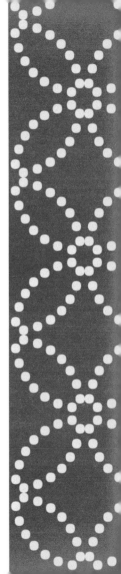

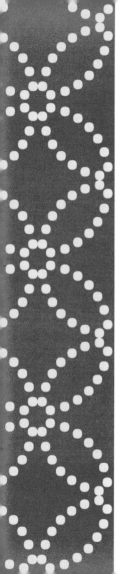

Life is not just a journey to the grave. It's an adventure to be set out on with courage and optimism.

Force of habit, or routine, can blind us to the wonders of the world around us.

To enjoy good health, to bring true happiness to one's family, one must first discipline and control one's own mind.

Buddha

Try to trust others; even if you are proved wrong, it will help to make you happy.

My advice to you is not to inquire why or whither, but just enjoy your ice cream while it's on your plate – that's my philosophy. **Thornton Wilder**

Truth is a deep kindness that teaches us to be content in our everyday life and share with other people the same happiness.
Khalil Gibran

To make a man happy, add not to his riches, but take away his desires.

Epicurus

The man who makes everything that leads to happiness depend upon himself, and not upon other men, has adopted the very best plan for living happily. **Plato**

Happiness is when what you think, what you say, and what you do, are in harmony.
Mohandas Gandhi

If we want to be happy, we need to put love first.

The best way to cheer yourself up is to try to cheer somebody else up.

Mark Twain

Happiness is neither virtue nor pleasure nor this thing nor that, but simply growth. We are happy when we are growing.
William Butler Yeats

Happiness comes when least expected; and departs just as suddenly.

**To have joy one must share it.
Happiness was born a twin.**

Lord Byron

When we recall the past, we usually find that it is the simplest things – not the great occasions – that in retrospect give off the greatest glow of happiness. *Bob Hope*

Beauty is the promise of happiness.

Edmund Burke

Happiness is a mystery, like religion, and should never be rationalized.

Gilbert K. Chesterton

Success is not the key to happiness. Happiness is the key to success. *Herman Cain*

I have learned to seek my happiness by limiting my desires, rather than in attempting to satisfy them.
John Stuart Mill

Happiness cannot be traveled to, owned, earned, worn or consumed. Happiness is the spiritual experience of living every minute with love, grace, and gratitude. *Denis Waitley*

Let someone know when you're happy, even if it's only yourself.

Knowledge of what is possible is the beginning of happiness.

George Santayana

There are as many kinds of beauty as there are habitual ways of seeking happiness.

Charles Baudelaire

Happiness is a choice that requires effort at times. *Aeschylus*

The greater part of our happiness or misery depends on our dispositions and not our circumstances.

Martha Washington

Happiness is like a butterfly which, when pursued, is always beyond our grasp, but, if you will sit down quietly, may alight upon you.

Nathaniel Hawthorne

Happiness is a thing to be practised, like the violin. *John Lubbock*

The best remedy for those who are afraid, lonely, or unhappy, is to go outside, somewhere where they can be quiet, alone with the heavens, nature, and God. Understand that the right to choose your path is a sacred privilege. Use it. Dwell in possibility. *Oprah Winfrey*

The best remedy for those who are afraid, lonely or unhappy is to go outside, somewhere where they can be quite alone with the heavens, nature and God. Because only then does one feel that all is as it should be and that God wishes to see people happy, amid the simple beauty of nature.
Anne Frank

There is only one happiness in life, to love and be loved. *George Sand*

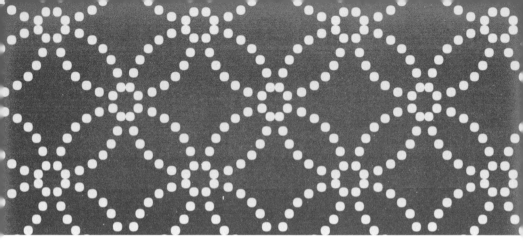

Try to focus on the present, otherwise you'll miss the good stuff – the here and now!

You don't have to go anywhere to get somewhere.

A true friend laughs at your jokes when they're not very good, and sympathizes with your troubles when they're not very bad.

Every path has its puddle.

Be more fully aware of what is all around you – what you can see, hear, touch, and taste.

Nothing ventured, nothing gained.

Have a kindness day – one day a week, try to perform at least five different acts of kindness for different people.

We have eyes to see the beauty of all that is around us … ears to hear the music of nature … and feet to feel the grass grow …

Don't take your relationships for granted. They need to be nurtured, like a garden of flowers.

Positive emotions nourish us.

Be frivolous from time to time. It's essential!

Discover what makes you come alive, and bring more joy into your life.

If you feel blocked and frustrated in life, write down the problems you have. It will clear your head, and help you to move on.

Spirituality has three stages: discovery, practice, and struggle.

What do you hold sacred in your life? Whatever it is, nurture it …

If you feel down, be honest with yourself and think about why. And then move on.

Make sure you stop to help others as you travel along your way.

Go forward, go sideways, go upwards. Just don't go backwards.

Travel will take your mind off your cares, if you are lucky; but sometimes, you can find paradise right where you are.

As you walk along, notice how the soles of your feet touch the ground. When your mind begins to wander, bring it back to this simple activity.

Happiness is a skill we can learn.

Do not be overshadowed by the mountains all around you. Instead, take pleasure in the peaceful valley that you find yourself in.

Don't be afraid to be assertive. People can cope with conflict if they know that it can be resolved peacefully.

Of all the things you wear, your expression is the most important.

Janet Lane

A truly happy person is one who can enjoy the scenery while on a detour.

Happiness held is the seed;
happiness shared is the flower.

The best vitamin to be a happy person is B1.

Happiness is a field you can harvest at every season.

When we pursue happiness,
we flee from contentment.

Don't worry, be happy.

Bobby McFerrin

Who cleans away every speck of dirt washes away happiness, too.

Happiness can grow from a tiny seed of contentment.

We would often be sorry if our wishes were granted. So be careful what you wish for!

Don't do whatever you like – like whatever you do.

When you are describing
A shape, or sound, or tint
Don't state the matter plainly
But put it in a hint
And learn to look at all things
With a sort of mental squint.

Lewis Carroll